The IEA Health and Welfare Unit

Choice in Welfare No. 38

Does Prison Work?

Charles Murray

Commentaries

Malcolm Davies
Andrew Rutherford
Jock Young

IEA Health and Welfare Unit
in association with *The Sund~· ~*
London

First published July 1997

The IEA Health and Welfare Unit
2 Lord North St
London SW1P 3LB

ISBN 0-255 36398-2
ISSN 1362-9565

Typeset by the IEA Health and Welfare Unit
in Bookman 10 point
Printed in Great Britain by
St Edmundsbury Press
Blenheim Industrial Park, Newmarket Road
Bury St Edmunds, Suffolk IP33 3TU

Contents

The Authors

Charles Murray is the author of *Losing Ground: American Social Policy 1950-1980*, 1984; *In Pursuit: Of Happiness and Good Government*, 1988; *The Bell Curve: Intelligence and Class Structure in American Life*, (with Richard J. Herrnstein)1994; and *What It Means to be a Libertarian: A Personal Interpretation*, 1997. He is the Bradley Fellow at the American Enterprise Institute, a public policy research institute in Washington DC.

Malcolm Davies is the Director of the Criminal Justice Centre in the Law School at Thames Valley University. He has conducted research on sentencing and penal policy in California, England and Finland. Currently he is engaged in a study of the attitudes of judges in five countries towards sentencing burglars. He is author of *Punishing Criminals: Developing Community-Based Intermediate Sanctions*, Greenwood Press: Connecticut, 1993, and joint author with Dr Hazel Croall and Jane Tyrer JP of the textbook *Criminal Justice: An Introduction to the Criminal Justice System in England and Wales*, Longmans: London, 1995, and more recently with Jane Tyrer and Jukka-Pekka Takala he published *Penological Esperanto and Sentencing Parochialism: A Comparative Study of the Search for Non-Prison Punishments*, Dartmouth: Aldershot, 1996.

Andrew Rutherford is professor of law and criminal policy at the University of Southampton. Since 1984 he has been chairman of the Howard League for Penal Reform. His recent books include *Transforming Criminal Policy*, Winchester: Waterside Press, 1996, co-editor of *Capital Punishment: Global Issues and Prospects*, Winchester: Waterside Press, 1996; and editor of *Criminal Policy Making*, Aldershot: Dartmouth, 1997.

Jock Young is Head of the Centre for Criminology at Middlesex University. He was born in Scotland and educated at the London School of Economics. Professor Young's books include *The New Criminology*, with P. Walton and I. Taylor, Routledge, Kegan, Paul, 1973; *The Islington Crime Survey*, Gower, 1986; *Losing the Fight Against Crime*, with J. Lea and R. Kinsey, Blackwells, 1986; *What is to be Done About Law and Order?*, with J. Lea, first edn., Penguin, 1984, second edn., Pluto, 1993; and *The New Criminology Revisited*, with P. Walton, Macmillan, 1997.

Foreword

Charles Murray's *Does Prison Work?* is a longer version of an essay that appeared in two parts in *The Sunday Times* during January 1997, and we are very grateful to the Editor, John Witherow, for granting permission to re-produce the material.

Previous IEA publications by Murray, about 'the underclass', were accompanied by critical commentaries as an aid to teachers who wanted to acquaint their students with more than one point of view. *Does Prison Work?* continues this tradition and contains three essays by leading academics.

Professor Andrew Rutherford, from the University of Southampton, has been Chairman of the Howard League for Penal Reform since 1984. He puts the view of the anti-prison establishment, whose ascendancy over recent decades Murray is criticising.

Professor Jock Young, of Middlesex University, was among the first criminologists to break ranks with those sociologists who argued that crime was not really rising. The 'new realism' of Professor Young acknowledged that rising crime was a fact, and not merely the perception of people in a state of 'moral panic'. However, he disputes Murray's claim that increasing the risk of imprisonment reduces criminal conduct and points to experience in some European countries that does not match the American evidence cited by Murray.

Professor Malcolm Davies, of Thames Valley University, shares Murray's general view, but shows that he could have advanced a stronger criticism of judicial sentencing. Murray compares 1954 (when about 21 per cent of offenders found guilty of an indictable offence were sentenced to custody) with 1994 when the proportion was 17 per cent. But Professor Davies highlights the fluctuations that occurred during the intervening years. The use of imprisonment fell from the early 1950s to a low of 12 per cent in 1973, rising to 18 per cent in the mid-1980s, before falling again to a low of 14 per cent in the early 1990s, only to increase to 20 per cent in 1995.

Between them, Charles Murray and his critics have provided a succinct introduction to the issues that, to this day, divide judges, criminologists and public policy-makers.

David G. Green

Does Prison Work?

Charles Murray

1. The Great Decline in Imprisonment

In 1955, crime began to get safer in England.

No one noted it at the time. The only way to tell that anything had happened was to rummage through crime statistics that wouldn't be published until a few years later. Even then, the evidence involved such a small event that it ordinarily wouldn't be worth mentioning. What happened between 1954 and 1955? The ratio of prisoners to crimes dropped slightly.

This minor event becomes significant only in retrospect. It was the beginning of a sustained decline in the use of imprisonment that continued with only a few short interruptions for 38 years. During the period of the Great Decline, the number of reported crimes increased twelvefold, while the number of prisoners only doubled.[1] Put such trends together, control for the size of the changing population, and the result is dramatic, as shown in Figure 1.

This is not some minor change in policy of interest only to criminologists. The risk of going to jail if you committed a crime was cut by 80 per cent.

The reduction varied from crime to crime. In 1954, the number of people sentenced to prison or borstal for felonious wounding represented one out of five such felonious woundings; in 1994, one out of eight—a drop of 45 per cent.[2] For rape, the number of people sentenced to custody went from one out of three rapes to fewer than one out of twelve—down 77 per cent. For burglary, from one out of ten to one out of a hundred—down 87 per cent. For robbery, from one out of three to one out of twenty—down 86 per cent.

1

Figure 1
The Great Decline in Imprisonment, 1950-1995

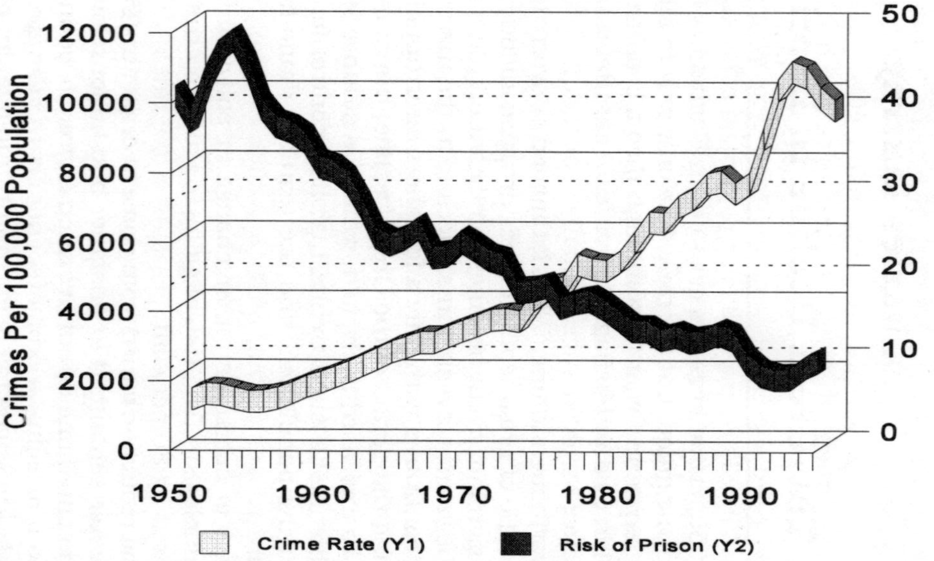

Prisoners Per 1,000 Crimes

Crimes Per 100,000 Population

Crime Rate (Y1)

Risk of Prison (Y2)

This is a matter of arithmetic, not ideology. Whether your politics are left-wing or right-wing, it is a fact undeniable that crime has gotten safer for the criminal in the last forty years. Furthermore, it is a situation that remained essentially unchanged in 1996. Michael Howard's 'prison works' policy represents a major change in the direction of English criminal justice, but look at the right-hand edge of the trendline for imprisonment. The risk of going to prison has still been barely nudged.

Why did the Great Decline begin? Not because there weren't enough cells for prisoners. At the outset of the Great Decline, the raw number of prisoners was falling. Throughout the first decade of the decline, the increases in crime were slow enough that England could easily have maintained a constant risk of going to prison if that's what the criminal justice establishment had wanted.

But the establishment did not want to maintain a constant risk of going to prison. The fall in imprisonment reflected a quiet change in the élite wisdom about how to deal with crime. The 1950s saw the development of a broad consensus among criminal justice academics, then senior civil servants (the police largely excepted) that prison was retrogressive: A humane society should be able to find better ways of dealing with crime than locking people up. This consensus affected imprisonment policy informally from the mid-1950s. It eventually found expression in the Criminal Justice Act of 1967, which substantially lowered the length of imprisonment and increased the number of suspended sentences. In the 1970s and 1980s, even as the public began to become concerned about rising crime rates, the establishment viewpoint became more entrenched. It was shared by Home Office staffs under Conservative and Labour governments alike: prison is bad and counterproductive, to be avoided wherever possible. It prevailed as recently as the Criminal Justice Act of 1991. Even today, it seems fair to judge from Michael Howard's experience that he is fighting against the prevailing philosophy of the permanent staffs of the courts, the prison service, and the probation services.

Is the falling use of imprisonment to blame for rising crime? In the next chapter I will present the case for a qualified 'yes'. For now, I want to frame the debate with some more basics about *what* has happened to English criminal justice in the last forty years, putting aside for the moment the questions of why these changes occurred and whether they affected the crime problem. First, let us dispose of a few of the clichés about crime.

'Crime Rises Along With Modernity No Matter What Policies are Followed'

Of course crime has risen, goes this argument. It's the price of modernity. People now have autos and VCRs and colour televisions worth stealing, for example, whereas they didn't in earlier years. Of course theft and burglary have gone up.

The argument has always been glib. What is the obvious link between the march of modernity and rising violent crime, for example? Even when it comes to theft, the logic is dubious. Are we to believe that when people were much poorer than they are now, much more urgently in need of the bare necessities, that the incentives to steal were smaller than they are in the era of a generous welfare state? That a colour television is easier to steal in 1990 than money was in 1930? That a colour television is a more desirable object to an English youth of the 1990s than money was to an impoverished English youth of 1930?

In any case, the assertion that crime rises ineluctably with modernity is at odds with the facts, as demonstrated by England's own history. During the last half of the 19th century, English society underwent one of the most rapid, wrenching transformations from an agricultural to an industrial society that any nation has ever experienced—upheavals of a sort that would lead any modern sociologist to predict a spiralling crime rate. And yet the crime rate in London, the vortex of all this wrenching social change, dropped during the last half of the 19th century.[3]

Perhaps you prefer a more recent example. When Elizabeth II came to the throne in 1952—hardly a 'pre-modern' era in English history—crime was falling. There had been a rise in the crime rate through the 1930s and the war years, but it topped out in 1948. Over the next seven years, reported crime dropped by 16 per cent. More recently still, from 1993-95, England abruptly shifted from a steeply rising crime rate to three years of falling overall crime.

Or we may turn to what most readers probably assume is still the crime capital of the industrialized world, the United States. The fact is that most kinds of crime have been falling in the United States—not just for a few years but, albeit irregularly, since the beginning of the 1980s. Crime rates can and do remain steady or even fall in modern societies. It is worth enquiring why.

'Crime Hasn't Really Risen.
It's Just That More Crimes are Reported to the Police'

One hears this explanation repeated like a mantra in certain circles, but it's just not true. The Home Office has been tracking the total incidence of crime as opposed to reported crime since 1981 through the British Crime Survey (BCS). In 1981, 66 per cent of burglaries were reported—exactly the same percentage as in 1995.[4] Woundings? Forty per cent were reported in 1981, 39 per cent in 1995. Overall, 65 per cent of serious crimes were reported in 1981, compared to 67 per cent in 1995.[5]

The BCS has also demonstrated something that most of us know from our own experience: A large proportion of the so-called 'unreported crimes' are minor. Technically, they involve lawbreaking—the short scuffle in a pub, the flowers trampled by a trespassing youth, the CD taken from the front seat of your car when you left the window open. One doesn't think of reporting them to the police, but, if asked by a BCS interviewer whether you have had anything stolen, you might recall the purloined CD; asked if you have been assaulted, you might mention the lout who punched you in the pub. These incidents show up as 'unreported crime'. But they don't have the weight or feeling of a *crime* as most people use the word these days. Offences that are serious enough to result in a prison sentence also tend to get people excited enough to call the police.

Overall, from 1981 to 1995, reported crime increased by 91 per cent compared to a rise of 83 per cent as measured by the BCS. It is an interesting difference for scholars to explore; not a comforting difference for the public.

The BCS cannot take us back earlier than 1981. What about the rise in crime in the 1960s and 1970s? A school of thought, exemplified by the two-volume *Joseph Rowntree Foundation Inquiry into Income and Wealth* published in 1995, attempts to argue that the rise in reported crime during those decades was a statistical artifact.[6] According to this school, crime truly began to rise only after Margaret Thatcher arrived at Downing Street. The arguments such scholars must employ are inventive—it is not easy to explain away a quintupling of reported crime between

1950 and 1979 as a statistical illusion—but they do not with-
stand examination. There is no reason to think that the increases
in reported crime in the 1960s and 1970s were any less reflective
of increases in real crime than were the increases in reported
crime during the 1980s. I refer readers to Norman Dennis's
recent and devastatingly detailed commentary on the Rowntree
report in his book, *The Invention of Permanent Poverty*.[7]

Scholars' attempts to prove that the rise in crime during the
1960s and 1970s was only an illusion run into another problem:
There are too many people around who remember the 1950s. In
working-class neighbourhoods and council estates, some people
are old enough to remember a time when houses were safely left
unlocked and bicycles safely left unattended. They remember the
shock they used to feel when someone they knew experienced a
crime, or even experienced vandalism or gross incivility, so rare
were such events. The most plausible assumption should be that
unreported crime was *lower* in the 1950s than it was by the late
1970s; that, in earlier years, people were more likely, not less, to
call the police about the trespassing youth or the minor casual
theft. People who remember the 1950s know that crime was
already changing in the 1960s and 1970s. The scholarly debate
is finally catching up with the reality of lived experience.

Where Did the System Break Down?

The police catch the criminal; the prosecution obtains a conviction; the judge sentences. If the risk of being sent to prison goes
down, it is because something changes somewhere in this
process.

'The judges are to blame. These days, judges just slap criminals
on the wrist.' I will start with the last stage in the process,
because it contains the biggest surprise.

Judges in 1954 were unquestionably a tough bunch. If you
were found guilty in the assizes and quarter sessions, you ran
more than a two-out-of-three chance of a prison sentence for
most major offences.[8] Even a guilty verdict for 'larceny from
shops' had a 67 per cent imprisonment rate at the assizes and
quarter sessions. For felonious wounding and rape, the chances
of imprisonment went up to 79 and 80 per cent respectively.
Murder? If you committed a murder in 1954, you had better hope
that you were insane. Sixty people were committed for trial for

murder in 1954. Thirty of them were found insane. Of the twenty-five found sane and guilty, twenty one were sentenced to hang.

But, contrary to widespread belief, judges in today's England do not behave all that differently. All told, magistrates and higher court judges in 1954 sentenced offenders to immediate custody in approximately 21 per cent of the guilty verdicts involving indictable offences. In 1994, this figure had dropped to about 17 per cent. This represents a shift in policy (concentrated in the use of custodial sentences for offenders under the age of 17), but it is not the revolution in leniency that is often ascribed to today's courts.

Figure 2 shows the comparison for some major types of crime. The differences are very small for most categories. The only categories in which the change is noticeable are violence against the person and sexual offences, with 1994's judges being somewhat less harsh in one case but somewhat more harsh in the other. It remains true that life after a prison sentence has gotten noticeably easier in the last 40 years—offenders today serve a much smaller portion of their sentence than they used to. But the changed behaviour of judges in imposing prison sentences explains only a small portion of the drastic reduction in the risk of imprisonment.

'The police are to blame. They don't catch criminals the way they used to.' It's true; they don't. It is not surprising when one considers that the police have had to cope with a twelve-fold increase in reported crime since 1954, but the fact remains that a criminal faces a much lower probability of getting caught for most kinds of crime.[9] Figure 3 displays the comparison between 1954 and 1994.

The police still do almost as well as in 1954 for sexual offences and other crimes of violence against the person—partly because a high proportion of such crimes are committed by people who are personally known to the victim. But the graph also reveals signs that the police have been overwhelmed in the categories where the police must usually detect an anonymous culprit. The 1994 clear-up rates for burglary and theft were each little more than half of what they had been in 1954. The story for robbery was even worse. In 1954, police cleared up 51 per cent of all robberies; in 1994, that figure was down to 22 per cent.

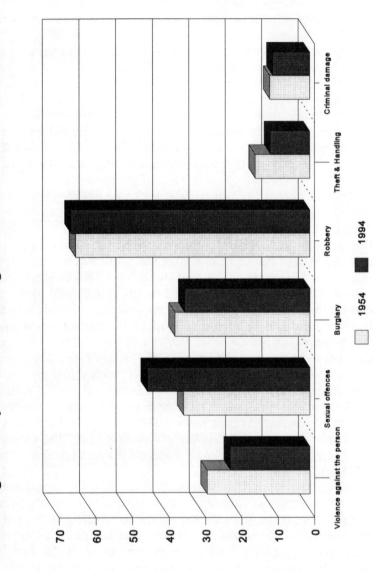

Figure 2

Percentage of Guilty Verdicts Resulting in Prison Sentences, 1954 and 1994

Figure 3
Percentage of Reported Offences Cleared up, 1954 and 1994

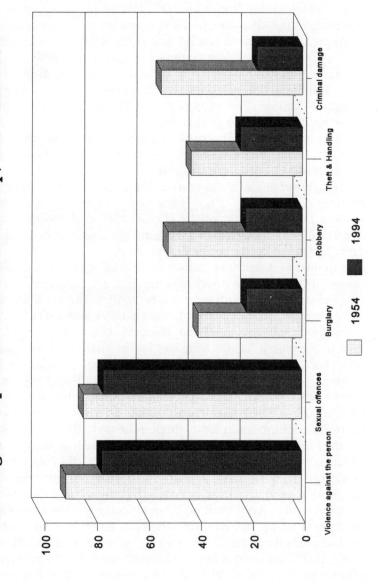

The more minor the crime, the greater the drop-off in police efficiency. English police in 1954 enforced all kinds of laws. For example, they cleared up 54 per cent of all cases of criminal damage to property (often, simple vandalism). By 1994, the police cleared up only 17 per cent of reports of criminal damage—and even that figure is exaggerated. It ignores cases in which the criminal damage was valued at less than £20, which are even more rarely cleared up. This bears on a topic to which I shall return subsequently: the 'broken windows' theory of crime, which says that one of the ways in which crime gets out of hand is when minor offences are ignored.

'The prosecutors are to blame. The police make an arrest, but nothing comes of it.' If one breakdown in the criminal justice system is to get most of the blame, this is it. Something has drastically changed between the time the police clear up a crime and the time a guilty verdict is reached.

Suppose we take the number of cleared-up crimes as the raw material given to the court system, and ask how many of these cleared-up cases result in a guilty verdict. Figure 4 shows the huge changes that occurred between 1954 and 1994.

For every category of crime, the odds you will be found guilty if you commit a crime *that the police clear up* have declined sharply. Consider robbery. In 1954, there were more guilty verdicts for robbery than there were cleared-up robberies (an oddity with several possible explanations, such as robberies cleared up in 1953 that came to trial in 1954 or conviction of more than one person for a single robbery). This much is sure: cleared-up robbery cases were pursued with a vengeance. In contrast, 1994 saw the police clear up 13,053 robberies, but convictions for robbery amounted to only 38 per cent of that figure. For some crimes, it appears that the system can barely be made to notice. Auto theft is the most conspicuous example. The police cleared up 103,378 auto thefts in 1994. But many of those were classified as 'unauthorized taking' of an automobile, which since 1988 has been a non-indictable offence. Of the indictable instances, a grand total of 2,118 persons were found guilty in 1994, roughly one out of every 50 cases in which somebody drove off with someone else's automobile and the police were confident that they knew who did it.

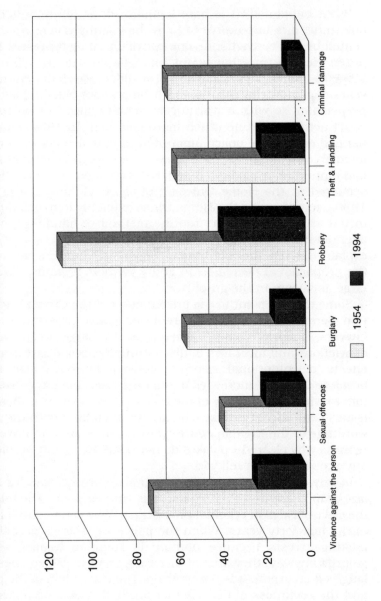

Figure 4

Percentage of Cleared-up Cases Resulting in a Guilty Verdict, 1954 and 1994

What happened? The bare statistics don't tell us much. For one thing, it is impossible to know how many crimes are represented by the convictions—one conviction may represent half a dozen cleared-up crimes. But this was as true in 1954 as in 1994, so it does not explain away the differences between the two years. We know that 'cautioning'—the practice of letting a known perpetrator go with a warning from the police but no further court action—became much more common. In 1954, cautions handed out by the police amounted to only five per cent of the indictable offences that the police cleared up. In 1994, that figure had more than tripled to 16 per cent. This increase in cautioning occurred at the Home Office's urging—beginning in the mid-1980s, for example, the Home Office explicitly instructed police to use cautioning as the routine method of handling juvenile offenders. But the increase in cautioning still leaves a lot to be explained. Even after subtracting offenders who were cautioned, the proportional decreases in guilty verdicts remains nearly as large as shown in the graph.

Some experts point to the introduction of the Crown Prosecution Service in 1986, which replaced police prosecutors with lawyers, followed shortly thereafter by large decreases in convictions and increases in discontinued cases. Apart from the effects of intentional reforms, convictions have also fallen because the large increases in offences often force the prosecutors to winnow out many of the less serious cases. But these are issues I will leave to those who are more familiar with the inner workings of the English court system. There are a multitude of reasons why cleared-up cases do not result in a guilty verdict, as any prosecutor can tell you.

In any case, I am not indicting English prosecutors for being lazy or indifferent, rather making this simpler point: The holes in the sieve of English criminal prosecution have gotten much larger in the last forty years. When the police say there's no point in making arrests because nothing is going to happen to the culprits anyway, they are not inventing excuses. When offenders laugh off an arrest, it is not bravado. The frustration of the police and the cockiness of the offender are both based on a realistic understanding of how the system now works.

What Else Could You Expect?

I promised to defer discussion of causation until the next section, but I will close with the obvious question. Imagine that in 1954 the Prime Minister had announced in a nationwide radio broadcast that England would establish a policy which, over the course of the next 40 years, would reduce the odds of a criminal going to prison by 80 per cent. 'That's daft,' all but the most starry-eyed idealists would have said. 'Crime will go through the roof if you do that.' That's what they would have said, and they would have been right. What else could you expect?

2. The American Experiment In Imprisonment

The broad proposition that 'prison works' is not in question. Of course prison can work, if it is used with sufficient ruthlessness. Can prison deter crime? Of course it can. If everyone who shoplifted were caught and immediately carted off to gaol for a year, shoplifting would become exceedingly rare. Deterrence fails only because the odds of being caught and imprisoned aren't high enough, or because the sentence is not harsh enough. *Whether* prison can deter crime is not in question.

Can imprisonment prevent people from committing crimes? Of course it can. The technical term is 'incapacitation'. Burglars who are locked up don't commit burglaries. Rapists who are locked up don't commit rapes. Long prison sentences are especially effective in achieving incapacitation because crime is a young man's game. Incapacitation fails only because a criminal is imprisoned too late or let loose too soon, or because not enough criminals are imprisoned. *Whether* prison can incapacitate criminals is not in question.

But even if prison can work in theory, it doesn't necessarily work in practice. In the real world, given constraints of money and political will, is it realistic to hope that increasing the use of imprisonment will reduce crime?

The United States has conducted a haphazard natural experiment that helps to answer the question. Like England, it first tried a sustained, large-scale reduction in the use of prison. It then embarked on a sustained, large-scale increase in the use of prison that has lasted much longer and been much more massive than England's recent shift in prison policy.

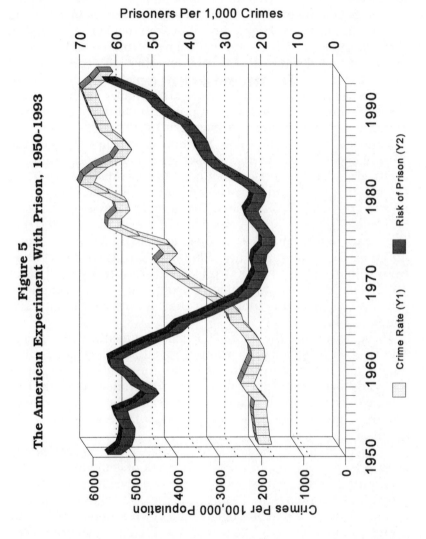

Figure 5
The American Experiment With Prison, 1950-1993

The great decline in imprisonment that occurred in England from 1955-1993 occurred much more precipitously in the United States. Beginning in 1961, the number of prisoners in state and federal institutions began an unbroken decline that lasted through 1968. It was not just a decline in the *risk* of imprisonment, but a decline in the raw number of people behind bars—and this while crime was growing rapidly. As late as 1974, the raw number of prisoners was still smaller than in 1961. Figure 5 shows the results when put in the terms of crimes per 100,000 population and prisoners per 1,000 crimes.[1]

Nineteen seventy-four saw the end of the first half of the natural experiment. America's experience had been the same as England's: Risk of imprisonment goes down, crime goes up. Then the reaction set in, and the United States began sending criminals to prison in wholesale lots. The number of prisoners in state and federal prisons in 1974 stood at 218,205. It reached 300,000 five years later, in 1979. It took four more years to reach 400,000, three more to reach 500,000. Since then, the US has been adding about 100,000 prisoners every two years. As of 1995, more than a million people were in American prisons—considerably more than that, if one adds in city and county gaols.

These figures are the stuff of horrified commentary in Europe. The US has a higher proportion of its citizens locked up than almost any other country in the world. America still has one of the world's highest crime rates. QED: Prison doesn't work. But this neat formulation is inaccurate. In reality the US experiment has three quite different lessons to teach the rest of the world about prisons.

Lesson 1: When crime is low and stable, it is a catastrophe to **stop** *locking people up.* In England the risk of going to prison for committing a crime fell by about 80 per cent over a period of forty years. In the United States, starting in 1961, it fell by 64 per cent in just 10 years. Whereas England slid down a slope, the United States jumped off a cliff. Whereas the English crime rate rose gradually, the US crime rate shot up.

It is important to pause and clarify an issue of causation. If crime shoots up, the rate of imprisonment may lag behind just because the system cannot keep up. But that's not what happened in the United States. In the US in the early 1960s (as in England in the mid-1950s), the use of imprisonment began to drop before increases in crime prevented the system from keeping up.

By the time the US started increasing the numbers of people in prison in the mid-1970s, huge increases were required just to make the risk of imprisonment keep up with the continuing increases in crime. Only in the last few years, with more than a million people in prison, has the ratio of prisoners to crimes reached the level that prevailed in 1961. Using a more sophisticated measure of the risk of imprisonment called 'expected punishment', economist Morgan Reynolds has calculated that the expected punishment for committing any one crime in 1986, after ten years of steeply rising prison populations, was still only 19 days, about one-fifth of the 93 days that an offender could expect as his punishment for committing a crime in 1959.[2] It is easy to maintain a low crime rate and a high risk of imprisonment. It is agonizingly difficult to try to re-establish a high rate of imprisonment after crime has been allowed to get out of hand.

England is learning this lesson for itself. To re-establish the ratio of prisoners to offences that prevailed in 1954, England would have to quintuple the prison population. This is not going to happen. Michael Howard's policies, which have caused such a furor, have resulted so far in a 25 per cent increase in annual prison receptions from 1992 to 1995, and only a 14 per cent increase in the average daily prison population. These increases have returned the risk of crime all the way back to the level that prevailed in ... 1989.

Lesson 2: Prison can stop a rising crime rate and then begin to push it down. The American crime rate hit its peak in 1980, a few years after the risk of imprisonment had bottomed out. Since then, with only a few exceptions, rates for the various serious crimes have been retreating in fits and starts to levels of twenty or more years ago. As of 1995, property crime is back at the rate it first reached in 1975, with burglary down more than 40 per cent from its peak. The homicide rate is lower than it has been since 1969. Robbery has bobbed up and down within a narrow range for twenty years. In 1995 it stood at the rate it first reached in 1975. Only one major type of violent crime, aggravated assault (roughly comparable to England's 'wounding'), is still near its peak, and even aggravated assault has been dropping for the last three years.

The academics are still arguing about how much of the overall reduction in crime can be attributed to the increased use of prison. For many years, the received wisdom in the United States and England was the same: not much. Changes in the demographics of the population were given most of the credit. But in the last several years, study after study has indicated that prison has played a crucial role. The most recent of these appeared in the May 1996 issue of the *Quarterly Journal of Economics*—hardly a mouthpiece for the pro-prison lobby—written by a Harvard economist, Steven Levitt.[3] Levitt concluded that a 1,000-inmate increase in the prison population prevents about 4 murders, 53 rapes, 1,200 assaults, 1,100 robberies, 2,600 burglaries, and 9,200 larcenies. The summary of the trade-off: about 15 crimes eliminated for the cost of incarcerating one felon, making imprisonment cost-effective by any method of calculating the cost of crime. Another analysis of these data argues for even larger effects of prison—21 crimes, not 15, are prevented per additional prisoner.[4] Patrick Langan, a senior statistician at the Bureau of Justice Statistics, has concluded that the increase in the American prison population from 1975 to 1989 probably reduced violent crime by 10 to 15 per cent of the figure it would have been, thereby preventing a 'conservatively estimated 390,000 murders, rapes, robberies and assaults in 1989 alone'.[5]

Scholars can reach such conclusions by comparing offenders who are left on the streets with offenders who are imprisoned. Despite America's current reputation for sending everyone to prison, over 60 per cent of American defendants accused of violent felonies are released while awaiting trial.[6] About half of all persons convicted of a violent offence are not sentenced to prison. Criminals imprisoned for violent crimes serve an average of less than half their terms. And these statistics apply to violent offences. For property offences, the system is far more forgiving. The result is that scholars have a rich supply of criminal behaviour to study among people who could be in jail but aren't. The findings are frightening.

For example, a federal study of state prisoners found that 45 per cent of them were in prison for a crime they had committed while on probation or parole. Most of those on probation had never been in prison (one cannot invoke the 'prison-only-makes-them-worse' argument to explain their behaviour). Counting only the crimes for which they were sent to prison, the 162,000 probation violators in the study accounted for 6,400 murders, 7,400 rapes, 10,400 assaults, and 17,000 robberies. Based on everything we know about chronic offenders, these numbers would be some magnitude larger if we could add in the many unapprehended crimes that these probationers committed. The comparable statistics for crimes committed by convicted felons while they were on parole from prison are comparably depressing.

The American criminal justice system leaves criminals on the street every day. American citizens, disproportionately low-income black Americans, pay the price. One is asked why America insists upon locking up so many people. I am reminded of Maurice Chevalier's answer when asked if he minded growing old: 'Not when I consider the alternative.'

Lesson 3: Prison is no panacea. It is true that US crime has receded during the 1980s and 1990s, but it is still extremely high compared to the 1950s. The increased use of prison contained the invasion, but it has not won the war.

Nor is it likely to. Raising the imprisonment rate does not affect many of the 'root causes' of crime. Just what those root causes might be is the subject of lively debate, but the idea that a rising crime rate has important causes other than changes in the threat of punishment is valid. Most people refrain from stealing things even when they know they could get away with it, and likewise refrain from settling their arguments by clubbing the other fellow over the head. They are acting out of habits of thought and behaviour inculcated from youth—the habit of virtue, to invoke Aristotle—rather than from a day-to-day calculation of their odds of getting caught and sent to prison. The habit of virtue has eroded in England as in the United States, and the reasons for its erosion must be reversed if crime is to retreat to 1950s levels.

The left attributes the erosion of virtue to such causes as poverty, social inequality, and various other ravages of capitalism. Others, including me, attribute it to the welfare state and an attendant culture that relieves people of accountability for their behaviour. The whole truth is doubtless more complicated than any one explanation can encompass. But for practical purposes it makes little difference who is right. The political will to do much about any of the big forces at work does not exist. England is not going to give socialism a second chance as the left wishes nor will it dismantle the welfare state as I wish. Whatever the social forces that produce amoral, unsocialized, unmotivated new generations of low-income youths may be, they will continue. If you are looking for a return to 1950s crime levels through increased prison, you are going to be disappointed.

What Do We Want Prison to Accomplish?

So incarcerating people will not, by itself, solve the crime problem. But an intelligent approach to prison does not require that it do so. A leading American criminologist, John DiIulio, weary of hearing the critics of prison repeat that 'Incarceration is not the answer,' got to the heart of the matter: 'If incarceration is not the answer,' he wrote, 'what, precisely, is the question?'[7]

If the question is, 'How can we restore the fabric of family life and socialize a new generation of young males to civilized behaviour?' then prison is not the answer. If the question is, 'How can we make unemployable youths employable?' prison is not the answer. If the question is 'How can we rehabilitate habitual criminals so that they become law-abiding citizens?' prison is only rarely the answer.

But if the question is 'How can we deter people from committing crimes?' then prison is an indispensable part of the answer. If the question is 'How can we restrain known, convicted criminals from murdering, raping, assaulting, burglarizing, and thieving?' prison is by far the most effective answer short of the death penalty.

3. Making Prison Work

Jim Doyle, a retired artisan who has lived in an inner-city council estate in Manchester since 1962, has watched crime grow from a rarity into part of everyday life, and he's angry: All the police are bald headed, he says. 'Bald headed?' I ask. From tearing their hair out. 'The courts say "Don't be a naughty boy"'—Doyle makes a motion of slapping a wrist—'and the police see this and say, "What am I doing this for?" The lads are laughing at them'. Doyle, head of a tenants' committee, once had a chance to say as much to Lord Justice Woolf, of the famous Woolf Commission. 'The courts have not got a clue!' he says he told Woolf. 'Get out of your country houses and come live around here!'[1]

To an American observer, it is all very familiar. The English public, like the American public, sound angry, frustrated, and ready for a tough approach to crime. It's not just the Jim Doyles, living in rough council estates. As people in all social classes have to modify their lives to cope with crime, the anger about crime has become general. The English police, like American police, mostly agree with the public. And yet, somehow, not much seems to change.

More has changed in the United States than in England. The sheer magnitude of the American increase in imprisonments is evidence of that. But American reforms have been hard won against determined resistance. A large and influential portion of the American judiciary remains philosophically opposed to tough sanctions on crime, and overloaded prosecutors let large numbers of serious offenders slip through the cracks as a way of keeping the system afloat.

In the case of England, the philosophical opposition is much more widespread than in the US, extending throughout the system (largely excepting the police), and the overload is just as great. Result: Michael Howard came to the Home Office, a vocally

21

law-and-order Conservative party had governed England for fourteen years—during which time it enacted a series of changes in practice that could have come straight from the textbooks of the most conventional academic criminologists. More use of the caution, less use of prison, shorter time served, more permissive parole and probation.

The establishment's disdain for the public's view of crime can be breathtaking. A leading case in point is David Faulkner, Deputy Under-Secretary of State at the Home Office until 1990. Writing in *The Guardian* earlier this year, Faulkner charged that Michael Howard's abrupt shift in prison policy had left a 'void at the centre of the criminal justice system'. Then came this astonishing statement: As a result of Howard's reforms, Faulkner wrote,

> *The police are unsure whether their main task is simply to detect and arrest criminals*—or whether they have a wider social purpose in maintaining social stability and confidence, in tackling crime by other means, or in protecting individual rights and civil liberties.[2]

This is the considered opinion of a senior criminal justice official in a Conservative government—proud of correcting the outdated notion the main task of the police is to detect and arrest criminals. The untutored public may ask if it isn't precisely by detecting and arresting criminals that the police maintain social stability and confidence; if it isn't by making the streets unsafe for criminals that the police chiefly protect rights and civil liberties. But to people of Faulkner's mindset—'We know better'—such responses are hopelessly Neanderthal.

That mindset is not rare. At an off-the-record lunch while I was in England, an important figure in the judiciary was outraged that Michael Howard's position on prison had become 'respectable'. Even worse, the official observed, Labour was sounding as bad as the Tories on crime, eager to pander to the electorate for political advantage. 'It is very sad.' Issues such as crime and prisons should 'be taken off the political agenda altogether', so that the professionals could deal with them dispassionately and correctly.

I should emphasize that such open disdain for the public was exceptional. The probation officers, prison officials, and judges whom I met during an unsystematic tour of the English criminal justice system were generally sympathetic toward the public's concern—and impressively professional. If I am ever to be tried and locked up, I hope it is by English courts and jailers. But their sympathy was that of the physician for an hysterical patient. At every turn there remained a large degree of the 'we know better' attitude, more nuanced and more gently expressed: The public is unduly worried about crime and too easily led astray by simplistic appeals to 'lock 'em up'. Let the experts take care of it.

In this stand-off, the criminal justice establishment and the public each has some large truths on its side. Ideology aside, the establishment is right to point to the practical difficulties of enforcing a lock-'em-up policy on a large scale. If the statistics show that most people who are arrested once are not arrested again, does one really want to throw first-time offenders into gaol? Is it worth spending many thousands of pounds per year to put a petty thief behind bars? The establishment is also correct when it predicts that a tougher policy will not have huge effects on the crime rate. England can hope for the same kind of effect the US has achieved—a significant dampening effect on crime, but probably not a dramatic transformation for the better.

Meanwhile, the public has hold of an even larger and more important truth: The risks of criminal activity are low. Large numbers of criminals are getting away with crime and then continuing to prey on their neighbours.

Let me suggest approaching the crime problem from a different direction. Perhaps no one knows how to drive the crime rate down to 1950s levels, but reducing crime is not the only measure of success for criminal justice policy. The public is not upset about the crime problem only because the crime rate has gone up. Much of the public's anger and anxiety arises from two other aspects of the crime problem: a breakdown in lawfulness and a breakdown in public civility. Both can be restored, whether or not serious crime goes down.

Lawfulness

'Lawfulness' does not necessarily mean a low crime rate. Rather, lawfulness means that *predatory behaviour is treated in a predictable and understandable way that corresponds with commonly shared principles of right and wrong within the community*. Crime exists and is part of life. Lawfulness doesn't require that no one is ever burgled. But lawfulness does require that the police look for the burglar, even if they can't catch him. If the police catch him, the prosecutors may not be able to convict, but they have to prosecute. If the verdict is guilty, the judge does not need to put the burglar behind bars for life, but the sentence must represent real punishment.

A criminal justice system that does all of these things predictably and reliably will go a long way toward re-establishing confidence in the lawfulness of daily life. It will also probably cut the crime rate, but cutting crime is a separate goal. The point of a lawful criminal justice system is that it does *not* make decisions on the basis of whether they are expedient. A lawful court doesn't cut corners because it doesn't have enough money to do what it ought. It doesn't act as a helping hand for the misguided or disadvantaged. The court engages in a solemn truth-seeking process. It is a stage in a never-ending morality play. It is the public forum in which the peaceful members of the community assert their supremacy over the outlaws. It dispenses just deserts.

Public Civility

The breakdown in public civility seldom involves serious crime. It means putting up with walls defaced with graffiti, stepping around vagrants sprawled in doorways, passing by knots of verbally abusive adolescent males, having to grope your way up a darkened council estate staircase because the light fixtures have been broken by vandals.

Graffiti is a minor offence. So is being drunk in public, littering, breaking light bulbs, or yelling obscene remarks at passers by. But these behaviours decisively affect the quality of life for people who have to live with such behaviours every day. They also prepare the way for serious criminality. This is the 'broken windows' hypothesis originated by American political scientists James Q. Wilson and George Kelling.[3]

If a window in a building is broken and left unrepaired, Wilson and Kelling pointed out, you can be sure that soon every other window will be broken as well. So too, as the small offences are ignored, the social controls for maintaining public civility erode. People who used to enforce the local norms move out or withdraw from neighbourhood life. Drug dealers and prostitutes operate in these dishevelled neighbourhoods, not in the well-tended ones. It is in neighbourhoods where no one cares about the little offences that a car left unattended will be stripped, and that teenage boys will seize a target of opportunity and rob—first as a lark, then purposefully. A war against crime must begin, not end, with enforcement of the basics of public disorder.

Wilson's theory has been recently getting a practical test in a number of US cities, most famously New York, where police set about energetically enforcing the little laws in some of the city's toughest neighbourhoods. The results have been spectacular—New York City saw a 37 per cent drop in serious crime and a 50 per cent drop in the homicide rate during just three years in the mid-1990s.[4] The jury is still out on precisely how much of this improvement may be attributed to the broken windows strategy, but it already seems likely that it played a major role. But as in the case of lawfulness, reducing crime is a separable issue. Restoring public civility produces a good in itself, making daily life much more liveable.

Coming to Terms with the Young Offender

How does one go about restoring lawfulness and public civility?

The first steps must begin with the young offender. 'Young offender' can mean anyone under 21, but the need for reform applies most emphatically to offenders under the age of 18, who now account for upwards of a third of all serious crime and a much higher proportion of offences against public civility.

For more than three decades, English criminal justice policy has taken successive steps to make the criminal justice system less punitive toward youngsters. The motives were noble, but the effect has been that young offenders can be confident that not much is going to happen to them for any offence short of a major felony—and maybe not even then. This is particularly true of offenders in their early teens. Only 10 per cent of all youths aged under 14 who were picked up by the police in 1994 for an indictable offence were even found guilty of anything, let alone given a meaningful punishment.[5] The rest were merely cautioned—let go, with no further action whatsoever, after a few minutes' lecture from a policeman. Compare this with 1954: Among those under age 14 who were picked up, 77 per cent were found guilty.[6]

Perhaps this statistic will convey the extraordinary change in England's behaviour toward the young offender: In 1954, a year when England experienced only one eleventh the number of indictable offences that it experienced in 1994, it found more than six times as many youths under the age of 14 guilty of indictable offences: 19,865 children in 1954 compared with 3,200 in 1994.

This does not mean that young offenders of 1954 were sent to jail in wholesale lots. Among youths defined as juveniles in 1954 (aged under 17) who were found guilty of an indictable offence, only eight per cent were sentenced to a residential facility—about the same percentage as in 1994, when nine per cent of youths under 18 found guilty were incarcerated (the age limit for 'juvenile' was raised to 17 in 1992).[7] The major difference between 1954 and 1994 is that in 1954 the system got tough with a few, but got stern with just about everyone—it called them to account—and did so very early in a youth's contact with the criminal justice system. In 1994, the system got tough with a few but did nothing to the many.

In certainly looks as if the old system worked. England of 1954 operated on the assumption that the best way to keep crime down was to intervene early and sternly. Crime was very low, and the number of youths picked up by the police went down by about half as children matured from their early teens to their late teens. England today operates on the assumption that the way to deal with crime is to be caring and forgiving of the young offender. Crime is very high, and the number of youths picked up by the police in 1994 roughly triples from the early teens to the late teens. The surviving members of 1954's England, looking at the results then and now, may be forgiven for concluding that they were right.

Enforcing the Rules for Everyone

Reform must begin with the young offender, but the general principles must apply to the whole system.

Restoring lawfulness means discarding most of the system's sympathy for the offender. A lawful system has only a minor interest in the reasons why someone commits the crime. The criminal justice system is there to punish the guilty, exonerate the innocent, and serve the interests of the law-abiding. Sympathy for the offender comes last.

Restoring lawfulness means drastically limited use of the caution. As a rule of thumb, the only offence appropriately cautioned is the one so minor that the victim wouldn't have bothered to report it if the police hadn't happened along.

Restoring lawfulness means charging defendants with the crimes they committed, not reaching agreements that let offenders plead guilty to lesser charges. By telling an offender (and the watching public) that he should treat the system as a game, plea bargaining—institutionalized in the US, informal but widespread in England—is perhaps the most corrosive of the modern practices of criminal justice.

Restoring civility means once again enforcing all the laws, including vagrancy, vandalism, trespass, and disorderly conduct. When people phone the police for such minor offences, they must be confident that the police will arrest and that the courts will convict.

Restoring both lawfulness and civility also means spending more money at every level of the criminal justice system— perhaps a great deal of money to pay for more police, more prosecutors, more courtrooms and, yes, more prisons. The price for letting crime get out of hand is high. The only choice is whether to pay it in the form of taxes or in the form of victims.

Old Truths

These observations, like others I have presented in this series, ride roughshod over many clichés about crime and prisons. 'Everyone knows' that arresting a youngster only labels him and makes him more likely to think of himself as a criminal. 'Everyone knows' that prisons only make people into smarter criminals, that prisons cost more than the crimes they prevent, and that the best way to reduce crime is to intervene as little as possible. Such clichés have been part of the received wisdom for so long that people assume there must be libraries of studies verifying them.

The opposite is true. Nothing has been more embarrassing to the keepers of the received wisdom than their inability to confirm their clichés with hard data. Nothing has been more infuriating to them than the accumulation of empirical evidence over the last few decades showing that crime is both deterred and prevented by the use of strict enforcement and meaningful punishment. The one success they can claim is to have kept the findings of that literature extraordinarily well hidden in the English debate about crime. The best thing that could happen to that debate is for politicians and academics alike to be forced to confront the scientific state of knowledge about crime and punishment.

That being said, the fundamentals about crime and punishment are not really mysterious. Human nature has not miraculously changed in the 20th century, nor have 20th century social scientists acquired insights into basic human motivations that had somehow previously escaped notice. As the technical literature grows on why people commit crimes, how they are deterred from committing crimes, and how they are made to desist from committing crimes, the core findings reaffirm a truth that humans have known since they first formed safe communities. Crime is low when crime doesn't pay.

Commentaries

Charles Murray
and the American Prison Experiment:
The Dilemmas of a Libertarian

Jock Young

The rate of crime is an inverse function of the chances of going to prison. What a simple formula and how easy could be the life of the criminologist if it were true! For the rates are, on the face of it, easily measurable and the nostrum which Charles Murray presents us with has a heavy leavening of common sense. Indeed, the graphs show quite clearly that crime rose in England and Wales as risk rates declined whilst the obverse occurred in the United States. The American experiment is thus seemingly a success story and the prison boat that arrived across the Atlantic, as I was writing this article, to be docked somewhat controversially in Portland Harbour, is a tangible export of American know-how and initiative when faced with the intransigent problem of crime.

Charles Murray is a brilliant polemicist; he has a knack of taking the conventional wisdoms of liberalism and dramatically 'proving' the converse. He has done this throughout his career: in *Losing Ground*[1] he lambasted the welfare state for generating 'welfare dependency', in *The Emerging British Underclass*[2] he argued that such dependency had generated an attendant culture where accountability for behaviour is undermined and the disciplines of family and community disintegrate, whilst in *The Bell Curve*,[3] written with Richard Herrnstein, he provocatively endorsed the existing social structure as increasingly reflecting differences in intelligences between classes and races rather than inadequacies in the meritocracy. How compatible these theories are with each other I am unsure. In the first book he has the poor as rational calculators evaluating the benefits of idleness as against work or crime as against honesty, in the second, in Murray's words, their 'habits of virtue' inculcated as youths are seriously eroded, in the last the poor are the lowest 'cognitive class' incapable of accurate assessment of risks and rewards. I sometimes test my students by calling them Murray I, Murray II and Murray III and ask them to try and draw lines of logic between them. On the face of it, they are not compatible. Each, for example, employs a divergent theory of crime. In the first crime occurs because of rational calculation, in the second it is because of lack of suitable upbringing (because of single mothers and feckless fathers), in the third delinquency occurs out of stupidity. In one the poor are rational calculators just like you or I (only poorer), in the second they actively endorse cultures which flirt with risk, in the last they are congenitally less aware of risk. Human nature may not have 'miraculously changed' in the twentieth century, as he argues in his conclusion (p. 28), but it seems to change within the corpus of his own work. But even more miraculous is this new book. For here, let us note, he starts off with a very strong statement of the inverse relationship between risk of imprisonment and crime, which is premised on the rational calculator (Murray I) but by the middle of his text his argument crumbles and Murray II emerges. (Murray III, thankfully, does not set foot in the argument.) For 'habits of virtue' have been irretrievably eroded and the threat of imprisonment, by page nineteen, is no longer a magic nostrum. It does not affect the root causes of crime, it will never result in a return to 1950s levels of virtue, it is rather a 'stand-off', an amelioration of a dire situation rather than a solution. For it is, he acknowledges, only by tackling the problems at source that crime rates can substantially be reduced.

But let us turn back to the strong version of his thesis, for this is the message that will surely grab the reader: namely, that there is a direct and obvious relationship between high risk of imprisonment and the level of crime. This formula is a classic of common sense, yet it is as incorrect as is its opposite, rather irritating, liberal assumption that the crime rate has nothing whatsoever to do with the imprisonment rate. Indeed, the fact that both beliefs exist side by side as self-evident in the public consciousness, allows Charles Murray the leverage to dismiss one by appealing to the, just as impossible, mirror opposite. At heart the problem is the recurrent notion that *the social is simple*. Namely, that the social world is a relatively simple structure in which rates of different social events (e.g. marriage, suicides, strikes, crimes) can be related to narrowly delineated changes in other parts of the structure. In fact the social world is a complex interactive entity in which any particular social intervention can only possibly have a limited effect on other social events and where the calculation of this effect is always difficult. Thus the crime rate is affected by a large number of things: by the level of deterrence exerted by the criminal justice system, to be sure, but also by the levels of informal control in the community, by patterns of employment, by types of child-rearing, by the cultural, political and moral climate, by the level of organised crime, by the patterns of illicit drug use, etc. etc. And to merely add together all these factors is complicated enough but insufficient for it does not allow human assessment and reflexivity—the *perceived* injustice of unemployment, for instance, or the *felt* injustices of bad policing or imprisonment. For the social is not only complex, like the natural world (who would ever think that only one factor would explain the weather?), it is even more intricate because each factor can be transformed over time by human interpretation. To take imprisonment, for example, the same sentence can be perceived by the individual as perfectly just ('I had it coming'), or as an unjust and unwarranted reaction to a petty crime which stokes up further resentment, leading to more serious crime in the future, or as a rite of passage which everyone in one's social circle goes through. Thus strange and distinctly unlinear relationships can occur. Low rates of imprisonment can act as an effective deterrent when the community is in accord as to the venality of the crime and the impartiality of the criminal justice system. In contrast, high rates of imprisonment can be counterproductive where they are seen as grossly unfair with regard to the level of gravity of the offence and the degree to which the system focuses on particular sections of the community rather than others.

All of this being said, it would be truly remarkable if there were to be found a simple relationship between risk of imprisonment and the rate of crime where there was a one-to-one relationship, with all other factors fading into the background. This is even more so given the timescale (1950-1990) which Murray takes to contrast the United States and Britain. This is a period which all social commentators agree has involved a battery of changes,

constituting perhaps the most significant structural transformation of industrial societies in the last hundred years. Patterns
of employment have changed, family and marriage have altered
ineradicably, the role of women has been transformed, youth
cultures have flourished, illicit drug use has spread, communities have disintegrated, the mass media has taken on a pivotal
role in our lives and—even factors which Murray has himself
stressed as relating to crime rates—the changing role of the
welfare state and the emergence of an underclass of the structur-
ally unemployed have occurred. And yes, *also* the risk of
imprisonment has changed. Surely it would demand a miracle for
one factor to override all these others, for all the factors to
change exactly in parallel in two very different cultures, and for
a simple inverse law to be so easily and unambiguously de-
tected? Yet, this is what Charles Murray asks us to believe in the
strong version of his thesis: with his dimmer switch theory of
crime, turn the risk of imprisonment up and the crime rates
fade.

Let us look at some of the evidence. At the very least one might
expect countries with high risks of imprisonment to have low
crime rates. The international comparison of crime rates is
notoriously difficult because of differences in definitions of
serious crime and the size of the hidden figure in each country.
But homicide figures are reasonably indicative, at least of levels
of violence. What are we to make then of the fact that the
imprisonment rate in the United States is over six times that of
Britain, and the risk of imprisonment per recorded crime over
eleven times, yet the homicide rate is seven times that of Britain,
as indeed it is of Switzerland which has an even lower rate of
imprisonment than Britain (40 per cent less), and, incidentally,
widespread gun ownership? The rational response to this must,
of course, be to move rapidly to a weak version of the thesis: to
say that the high crime rate of the United States relates to many
other factors rather than imprisonment and that the latter is only
one factor out of many.

But perhaps it is wrong to make comparison between countries given the flaky nature of the data. Isn't it better to look at
the impact of changes in risk of imprisonment over time within
countries where the definition of serious crime remains relatively
constant and all the other social factors are held, over a short

time, fairly constant? Alas, such comparisons give even less credibility to Murray's thesis. For example, between 1987 and 1995 the United States increased its prison population by 124 per cent and achieved a two per cent increase in crime, whereas Denmark increased its prison population by seven per cent and had a three per cent increase. Denmark has maintained a very low, fairly stable rate of incarceration in this period, a low risk rate of 0.6 prisoners per 100 recorded crimes and a low crime rate, whereas the United States has maintained an extremely high and rising rate of incarceration, a high risk rate and a high crime rate. At the moment the United States' incarceration rate is over nine times that of Denmark and its risk of imprisonment just under 20 times. Why, one might ask, are not hordes of American scientists and senators going off to Denmark to find out how the Danes got it right, and how they can find means of getting out of the vast and costly prison experiment which they have got themselves into?

And such examples could be multiplied: the Netherlands, for example, doubled its rate of imprisonment between 1987 and 1995 and the crime increase was only eight per cent. Surely, a success? Not really. Scotland, over the same period, had a four per cent increase in imprisonment and only four per cent increase in crime—half the increase of the Netherlands. Certainly this is a result which satisfies the virtues of value for money and efficiency which my countrymen are well known for!

Finally, let us look at an international comparison of European countries in the period of 1987-1995 in terms of risks of imprisonment and rates of recorded crime.

Risk of Imprisonment and Rate of Crime: Selected European Countries

1987-1995	% Change in Risk of Imprisonment	% Change in Recorded Crime
England and Wales	-17	+31
Scotland	0	+4
Republic of Ireland	-13	+20
France	-9	+16
Austria	-33	+24
Netherlands	+91	+8
Denmark	+4	+3

Risk of imprisonment is measured in terms of prisoners per 100,000 recorded crimes.

Note first of all there is a built-in tendency for the risk of imprisonment, when measured in terms of the number of inmates in proportion to the volume of crime, to decrease with any dramatic increase in the crime rate. The prison capacity can simply not keep up with the increase and, as Murray notes, this is particularly true when politicians are unconcerned with regards to the effectiveness of prison. The causality is, however, the reverse of Murray's: crime rises because of a host of factors and inevitably reduces the risk of imprisonment rather than a reduction in the risk of imprisonment bringing upon us the rise in crime. Such a tendency is particularly evident whenever the rise in crime is considerable, as in the case of England and Wales, the Republic of Ireland, France and Austria. But where crime rises are small, the failure of Murray's Law can be clearly observed. He focuses on England and Wales where it might seem self-evident, but in neighbouring Scotland the risk remains the same yet crime rises and in Denmark the risk rises and so does the crime rate, whilst in The Netherlands, to finally put the nail in the strong version of the thesis, the risk rate goes up exponentially but the crime rate continues to rise.

Let us begin to reformulate the thesis. The risk of imprisonment is certainly one factor that determines the crime rate, but it is one factor amongst many. Furthermore, it interacts with other factors: the cohesiveness of the community and the degree of legitimacy of the criminal justice system being obvious examples. Its effect, no doubt, varies by crime and by the subset of the community. Ironically, the white-collar criminal is more likely to be deterred by prison than the lower working-class youth with nothing to lose, who commits the sort of conventional crimes we send people to prison for. Risk rates, then, are important, but different groups will perceive the same risk differently. The prudent politician will hold such factors in mind just as he or she will be aware that to use one point of intervention as the major source of crime control is bound to have at some point declining marginal returns.

Murray's decision to focus so monopolistically on prison as a method of crime control stems possibly out of a fascination for the polemical, but it also arises out of a certain fundamentalism. He correctly notes that his present favoured formula fails to touch the root causes of crime: whether it be the left's belief in social inequality as a cause, or his belief in the welfare state and its attendant 'culture of dependency'. It matters not who is correct, he observes, because socialism is scarcely around the corner, nor the will to dismantle the welfare state as he would wish. I cannot see the logic in this, outside of the belief that without fundamental drastic change, nothing can be achieved. For there are many short-term and intermediate goals which can be realised: social inequality is not written in stone, it has decreased in the past and will decrease again in the future. And as for the welfare state, I doubt if advanced industrial societies are feasible without the underpinning of the welfare state, but our experience over the last twenty years has certainly shown that such a bedrock of decency can be undermined by determined forces of the right. What is most paradoxical is Charles Murray's fixation on the prison, given the publication of his recent lengthy personal document *What it Means to be a Libertarian*.[4] Why, one might ask, is a doughty libertarian like Murray advocating the American penal experiment when he also believes that it is not laws regulating automobile safety which affect the level of accidents, but rather the infrastructure of engineering improvements and that, amongst other things, air traffic control, drug regulating agencies, and anti-discriminatory measures should be taken out of state control? Why should such a staunch opponent of the State put his weight behind the greatest intrusion into the lives of citizens that has occurred in a mature liberal democracy?

Let us look at the enormity of the American experiment. The United States' prison population has more than doubled in the ten years from 1985 to 1995. There are now 1.6 million inmates, a population which, if brought together, would be the size of Philadelphia.[5] Furthermore, the imprisoned population is surrounded by a rapidly expanding penumbra of probation and parole. Now, one in thirty-seven of the American adult population is under some form of correctional supervision, a number which, if gathered together, perhaps for some administrative convenience, would consist of five million adults, and would easily be the second largest city in the United States.[6] It is not part of the social contract which underpins liberal democracy that it should imprison and oversee so many of its citizens. Nor is it that it should do so whilst being so palpably incapable of protecting them. The rates of violence in the Unites States are exceptional amongst the stable democratic societies: its overall homicide rate is seven times that of England and Wales, its murder rate for young men is a staggering fifty-two times higher, whilst large tracts of its major cities are no-go areas for its citizens, whether men or women.

The United States' crime rate has, of course, declined in the last few years, although in terms of violent crime, particularly homicide, it would be more correct to talk of a levelling out at a very high level. Thus the overall crime rate declined by three per cent between 1993 and 1995 but then the overall rate declined in twelve out of seventeen advanced industrial countries during this period.[7] It is certainly nothing to write home about and, even if this was due to the unlikely premise that such a decrease was predominantly due to imprisonment, it is difficult to imagine what size of prison population we would need to achieve Newt Gingrich's dream to bring the American rate down to European levels. Already some zealots such as John DiIulio are talking of doubling the prison population in order to combat crime.[8] It is difficult to see where this would end: a prison population the size of New York City, a correctional population the size of Los Angeles? Already some of our most perceptive social critics speak in Zygmunt Bauman's terms of a 'totalitarian solution without a totalitarian state'.[9]

Widespread alarm bells are set off by the extraordinary racial focus of this carceral experiment. Thus, one in nine of African-American males aged 20-29 is in prison at any one point and one in three is either in prison, on probation or parole.[10] These are staggering figures, even more so when we consider that they would increase drastically if we were to look at 'have ever' figures and if we were to focus on poor blacks rather than include the sizeable middle-class African-American community. There must be sizeable slices of the ghetto areas of the United States where a young man would be regarded as odd if he were not under some form of correctional supervision and any stigmatisation would probably be negligible; indeed it would be those untouched by the law who were regarded as strange. And yet despite this extraordinary level of risk of imprisonment, violence continues to decimate the black community and indeed increases. Homicide is the foremost cause of death amongst young black men in

America, just as imprisonment is the most likely career move in their lives; can there be any greater indictment of Murray's thesis than this?

Those of us in Europe who are friends of American democracy need to make clear our misgivings rather than import their mistakes. Our politicians, of course, of all perplexions, flit across the Atlantic to learn about this gross carceral experiment. But to attempt to learn crime control from the United States is rather like travelling to Saudi Arabia to learn about women's rights. The one lesson to be learnt is not to travel down this path of punishment, to realise that if it takes a Gulag to maintain a winner-takes-all society, then it is society that must be changed rather than the prison expanded.

Sentencing Trends and Public Confidence

Malcolm Davies

Charles Murray's article is about the general deterrent impact of imprisonment concluding that since the 1950s policy directions have been taken that have helped to promote rather than inhibit the growth of crime. The paper provides a critique of the prevailing prison reductionist and non-interventionist liberal orthodoxy that has helped to shape the penal paradigm over the last forty years.

Murray states the case for the theory of general deterrence, a theory which was at a low ebb following the 1990 White Paper's claim that:

> It is unrealistic to construct sentencing arrangements on the assumption that most offenders will weigh up the possibilities in advance and base their conduct on rational calculation.[1]

Murray argues that:

> incarcerating people will not, by itself, solve the crime problem ... But if the question is 'How can we deter people from committing crimes?' then ...prison is by far the most effective answer short of the death penalty (p. 20).

He states, 'Crime is low when crime doesn't pay' (p. 28) and cites the recent findings from the USA of Steven Levitt and the estimate that one incarcerated felon eliminates 15 felony crimes. The argument will run and run on the rates of recidivism, deterrence and the incapacitative effects of locking up criminals.

The empirical thesis of his argument is that for criminals the chance of going to prison has fallen dramatically in the period from 1954 to 1994. The prison reductionist claim about the overuse of custody is unconvincing when one contrasts, as Murray does, the steady but slow rise in prison population figures (doubled in 40 years) with the far more dramatic growth in crime over the period. Murray concludes, 'The risk of going to jail if you commit a crime was cut by 80 per cent' (p. 1).

The reduced risk of imprisonment was part of a policy switch towards diversion and tolerance of crime based on a variety of reasons that included the modernist assumption that prisons were outmoded and inhumane and the labelling theorists' concern to avoid stigmatising and hence reinforcing the offender's deviant behaviour. Thus prisons were considered as uncivilised by some prison reductionists and counter-productive by others. This approach is illustrated by the policies as regards younger offenders:

> For more than three decades, English criminal justice policy has taken successive steps to make the criminal justice system less punitive towards youngsters. The motives were noble, but the effect has been that young offenders can be confident that not much is going to happen to them for any offence short of a major felony (p. 25).

The prison as a place of rehabilitation was to give way to the view that prisons were counterproductive in rehabilitative terms, i.e. did not work and therefore we should minimise their use—a view espoused by Roy Jenkins when Home Secretary and his successors until Michael Howard.

Murray says: 'This fall in the use of imprisonment reflected a quiet change in the élite wisdom about how to deal with crime' (p. 3). The Advisory Council on the Treatment of Offenders (1944-1963) and the Prison Commissioners played their part in this quiet revolution which is commented on in the 1955 Annual Report of the Prison Commission:

> The Commissioners therefore in 1949 took a step which, though it passed without public notice, was of some significance for the development of their programme. They advised the Secretary of State to introduce into the Prison Rules which followed the Criminal Justice Act of 1948, certain Rules which were declaratory simply of spirit and purpose... 'The purpose of treatment and training of convicted prisoners shall be to establish in them the will to lead a good and useful life on discharge and fit them to do so.' Thus the principles of the prison system are now based not alone on the personal convictions of the Commissioners, which are at all times open to question, but on the sanction of Parliament.[2]

The shift in policy may have been a relatively quiet affair but Murray seeks to identify the agencies responsible for the decline in the chances of criminals going to prison in England and Wales. The police were in part to blame because of the fall in the clear-up rates for most crimes. Criminals have less chance of being caught today and if they are apprehended there has been a dramatic drop in the chances of being prosecuted and punished. The proportion of crimes cleared-up resulting in a guilty verdict has fallen as a result of cautioning and the discontinuation of cases by the prosecuting authorities. He says: 'When the police say there's no point in making an arrest because nothing is going to happen to the culprits anyway, they are not inventing excuses' (p. 12).

What is less convincing is his absolution of the judges and magistrates. Statistics presented in the May Report of 1979 show that in one decade the chance of being given a prison sentence for adult males convicted of indictable offences halved from over 400 per 1000 convictions in 1959 to 200 in 1969.[3] Christopher Nuttall and Ken Pease have plotted the reception of convicted prisoners from 1950 to 1991 and conclude:

> In the early 1950s about one processed offender in four was sentenced to immediate imprisonment... By the mid 1970s only one offender in 10 suffered that fate.[4]

Another way to look at sentencing trends is to examine all forms of custody used by the courts and include males and females of all ages who were sentenced for indictable offences. Figure 6 shows the percentage of offenders found guilty of indictable crimes from 1949 to 1995 who were given one of the following forms of custodial sentences for adults: imprisonment, corrective training (1949-1967), preventive detention (1908-1967), extended sentences (1967-1991) and the partially suspended sentence (1982-1992); and for younger offenders: borstal training (1908-1983), approved school order (1933-1970), detention centre order (1953-1988), youth custody order (1983-1988) and detention in a young offender institution (from 1988).

The percentages shown are based on data for males and females of all ages sentenced for an indictable offence in the higher criminal courts (the Crown Court replaced the assize and quarter sessions in 1967) or magistrates' courts and includes those sent to the higher court for sentencing after conviction in the magistrates' court.

The proportion of those given a custodial sentence fell from 21 per cent in 1954 to 12 per cent in 1973. Throughout the 1950s,

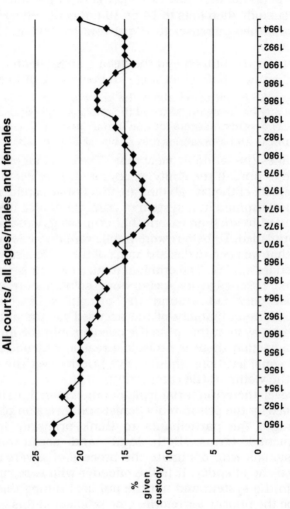

Figure 6

Percentage Use of Custody with Indictable Offenders 1949 to 1995 in England and Wales

All courts/ all ages/males and females

Source: Compiled from *Criminal Statistics England and Wales*, 1949 - 1995, London: Home Office.

of those convicted of an indictable offence, 20 per cent or more were given a custodial sentence. In contrast the rate from 1971 to 1980 ranges from 12 to 14 per cent. Figure 6 shows there is then a period of increase to 18 per cent in the mid-1980s. The use of custody then falls to 14 or 15 per cent between 1990 and 1993, and then increases to 17 per cent in 1994 and 20 per cent in 1995.

Whatever the outcome of the debate about sentencing trends Murray argues that something can be done about crime:

> The public is not upset about the crime problem only because the crime rate has gone up. Much of the public's anger and anxiety arises from two other aspects of the crime problem: a breakdown in lawfulness and a breakdown in public civility (p. 23).

He takes the laudable view that: 'The criminal justice system is there to punish the guilty, exonerate the innocent, and serve the interests of the law-abiding' (p. 26). Public confidence is likely to be undermined in a system of criminal justice if lawlessness is tolerated to such an extent that crime is ignored or criminals go unpunished. To help restore public confidence Murray is right to say that we need to discard 'most of the system's sympathy for the offender' (p. 26). The criminal justice system is not primarily designed to engage in social work solutions. It is first and foremost designed around the principles of retribution to establish the culpability of the accused for the offence. In an adversarial system this puts the offender into the limelight. But after conviction there is no logical reason why offender-instrumental considerations should have priority over the interests of either the victim or the community.

However the adversarial logic of our criminal justice system, reinforced by the prison reductionist and diversion philosophies, encourages the participants to think primarily in offender-instrumental terms. Both legal- and social-work-oriented professionals who dominate the process of adversarial justice focus on the offender. It is the offender who is regarded as the client in the system and not the public. Shifting this emphasis must be the priority for reform. One problem in this country that Murray identifies is that: 'The establishment's disdain for the public's view of crime can be breathtaking' (p. 22). How to maintain public confidence in the system of justice[5] as in Finland or incorporate a public input while avoiding the pitfalls of populist justice as witnessed in California[6] is a key issue.

Murray is correct to identify the important functions of sentencing in terms of just-deserts and denunciatory objectives. He says:

> The court ... is a stage in the never-ending morality play. It is a public forum in which the peaceful members of the community assert their superiority over the outlaws. It dispenses just deserts (p. 24).

Punishment in just-deserts terms is not an uncivilised idea. Citizens have a right to be protected in their homes and streets and just deserts require a notion of balancing the due process concerns of the individual accused of a crime with the community's need to identify and mark their intolerance of wrongful behaviour. While it is right for a judge to oversee the individual case and apply the tariff in the individual circumstances of a particular offence and offender, it must be right that in a democracy the general level of punishment is a matter of the wider public interest. The just-deserts tariff of punishments is not a technical matter that only can be decided upon by the judges and it is possible to conceive and implement a system of citizen consultation without handing over the process lock stock and barrel to voter referendums.

The Criminal Justice Act 1991 established a legislative framework based on just deserts and denunciatory principles. Within this framework prison can be regarded as working, regardless of its deterrent or incapacitative effects that Murray tries to establish, because it is accepted by the bulk of the public as a suitable institution for punishing people who have done wrong and have been convicted of a sufficiently serious crime such that imprisonment is justified.

My conclusion is that Murray's article is an important contribution to a debate that has become too focused on the consequences of sentencing on the offender. The effect of sentencing on the public in general, whether as potential lawbreaker or as an observer and participant in the 'never ending morality play' is something that has been disregarded for too long and has contributed to the problem of public confidence in the criminal justice system in this country.

Beyond Crime Control

Andrew Rutherford

In a critical appraisal of the Home Office, published in 1976, James Q. Wilson, the American political scientist, regretted 'the Americanization of English criminal justice'. He was dismayed that an unduly liberal stance by senior civil servants had resulted in them failing to learn from the mistakes made by their opposite numbers in the United States. Wilson declared that there was 'scarcely a single ill-advised recommendation of the President's Commission on Law Enforcement and Administration of Justice that the British Home Office and its various advisory councils do not seem determined to repeat.'[1] Wilson, who in earlier years had been an advisor to the Crime Commission and campaigner for Adlai Stevenson, was by then one of the nation's leading neo-conservative commentators, in no small measure due to his widely read and influential *Thinking About Crime*.[2] Twenty years later *The Sunday Times* commissioned another leading American conservative social theorist, Charles Murray, to look at crime and criminal justice in Britain. Murray is equally dismissive of what he views as the élitist mindset of officials such as David Faulkner who, as a Deputy Under-Secretary of State, was responsible for criminal policy at the Home Office between 1982-90 (p. 22). However, unlike Wilson, Murray is able to report that the cavalry has arrived just in time to rescue 'the risk of punishment' which he declares is rising although not to the nostalgic levels attained in the 1950s when people convicted of murder (guilty or otherwise) knew that they would surely hang.

The degree of Murray's debt to both Wilson and to John J. DiIulio (once Wilson's student and now his principal torchbearer) is impressive, and many of his assertions are a re-working of the prolific Wilson-DiIulio literature. Indeed Murray is something of an *arrivé* on the crime scene at this time and this is all the more curious as the issues have been so solidly reformulated by Wilson and his various disciples. In effect, there is precious little scope for a neo-conservative like Murray to do anything with criminal policy but to rework the same furrow. This arena, at least in the American context, hardly offers him the chance to redefine the public policy discourse as his *Losing Ground* did with the issue of welfare.[3] It may be that Murray and his ilk regard Britain, and no doubt other states, as relatively virgin territory, providing a degree of academic respectability to a course already set by the populist punitiveness of the mainstream political parties.

Charles Murray solemnly informs us that his conclusions are a matter of mathematics and not ideology. He is a mere social scientist following the data into the value-free environment of Harvard economists and number-crunchers working deep inside the Bureau of Justice Statistics at the United States Justice Department. This disclaimer is evocative of James Q. Wilson's assertion that he is neither a liberal nor a conservative but a pragmatist, interested only in the discovery of what works.[4] But Murray's neutral mathematics involve crucial decisions about how any calculations are to be conducted. At the heart of Murray's thesis lies a single question: over the last twenty-five years or so in the United States (or in Britain) has punishment increased or decreased? Between 1972-96 the number of people held in prisons and jails in the United States has more than trebled, and expressed as a rate per 100,000 inhabitants increased from 164 to 550. But for Murray, like DiIulio and others before him, this escalation of imprisonment, speaks not of severity but of softness. In 1994 DiIulio informed readers of *The Wall Street Journal* that:

> by every measure, the anti-incarceration élite has been winning its tug-of-war with the public on crime... America has crime without punishment.[5]

In similar vein, for Murray to describe increases in imprisonment as 'The Great Decline' is made possible by changing the denominator. As calculated by neo-conservatives, the prisoner rate per total inhabitants is disregarded and the general population is replaced by a figure which purports to be a measure of criminal events. This produces not an imprisonment rate but an index of 'risk of punishment'. If, for example, reported crime rises at a faster rate than prison usage by the courts, the risk of punishment declines and the wrong message is conveyed to criminals who are also engaged in similar calculations. Applied to the world of health care, this way of thinking would lead to a fourfold rise in hospitalizations being described as a reduction on the grounds that stress-related ailments have increased at an even faster rate. Furthermore, in this bizarre econometric neverworld, Murray would no doubt claim that this 'great decline' in hospital usage is leading to greater levels of stress. Any notions that there might be preventative strategies at the disposal of governments are also conveniently sidelined.

In the final analysis, it is not difficult to be left with the impression that the essence of Murray's concerns have rather less to do with crime control than with the expansion of prison and other control systems. For example, in endorsing Wilson and Kelling's 'broken windows' proposition and its 'zero-tolerance' implications for the police,[6] Murray gives priority to other public policy goals, namely those of lawfulness and public civility. As an advocate of the dismantling of public welfare services, the harsh winter of criminal justice is a necessary permanent accompaniment. At its core, the Wilson-DiIulio-Murray agenda for the new century is about the disposal, if not the elimination, of troubled and troubling people. In part, as John Gray has suggested, the destination being sought is Brazil with its brazen social exclusion. Other aspects evoke the social authoritarianism of Singapore and it does not seem far-fetched to talk of 'GULAGS, western style'.[7] Indeed the closest parallel may well be German criminal policy spanning 1933-38, and which included the first phase of concentration camps.[8] In marketing terms, there can be little dispute that the ideological right have prevailed within the American criminal policy arena and, over the last five years or so, in Britain. As Wilson cheerfully remarked in 1983, the differences in public discourse amounted to little more than a 'policy quibble'.[9] If the conventional model of criminal policy has been 'conservative', to follow Leon Radzinowicz's scheme,[10] that ground has now been decisively claimed for the 'authoritarian' model. As for the 'socio-liberal' model, although its plight seems ever more precarious, any eventual redefinition of criminal policy may well be in that direction. The few brave efforts of recent years[11] by no means represent the beginning of the end, but as Winston Churchill said in 1942 (thirty-two years earlier he had been, of all Home Secretaries, the one most firmly cast in the socio-liberal mould), they might just mark the end of the beginning.

Notes

Does Prison Work?

1: The Great Decline in Imprisonment

1   The ratio shown in the graph is based on average daily population divided by the number of notifiable offences. Daily population figures taken from Home Office, *Prison Statistics England and Wales 1995*, London: HMSO, 1996, Table 1.6, and comparable tables for prior years. The number of notifiable offences is taken from Home Office, *Crime Statistics England and Wales 1995*, London: HMSO, 1996, Table 2.2 and comparable tables for prior years, adjusted for changes in definitions of notifiable offences. I use the average daily population instead of the number of receptions during the calendar year because consistently defined data for receptions cannot be taken back as far as the data for average population. But it should be noted that for the overlapping period when both measures are available (back to approximately 1954), the relationship shown in the graph holds regardless of which measure is used.

2   All 1954 statistics, here and throughout the rest of the discussion, are taken from the 1954 volume of *Crime Statistics England and Wales*. Prison sentences aggregate the following categories. For sentences of magistrates courts: imprisonment without option of fine, detention centre, remand home, and approved school, as shown in Tables VII–X. For Assizes and Quarter Sessions: borstal training, corrective training, preventive detention, imprisonment, and death, as shown in Table III. All 1994 statistics, here and throughout the rest of the discussion are taken from the 1994 volume of *Crime Statistics England and Wales*. Imprisonment data for the categories of crime are taken from Table 7.2, for the category 'Total immediate custody.' For specific crimes (e.g., robbery, rape), the numbers were obtained through an unpublished breakdown of the 1994 statistics provided by the Home Office.

3   Gatrell, V.A.C. and Hadden, T.B., 'Criminal Statistics and Their Interpretation', in Wrigley, E.A. (ed.), *Nineteenth Century Society: Essays in the Use of Quantitative Methods for the Study of Social Data*, Cambridge: Cambridge University Press, 1972, pp. 336-96. Gurr, T.R., 'Contemporary Crime in

Historical Perspective: A Comparative Study of London, Stockholm, and Sydney', *Annals* 434, 1977, pp. 114-36.

4   For 1996 data, see Home Office, *The 1996 British Crime Survey*, London: HMSO, Table 2.3. For 1981 data, see Home Office, *The 1992 British Crime Survey*, London: HMSO, Table A2.5.

5   *The 1996 British Crime Survey*, Table 2.1.

6   Income and Wealth Inquiry Group, *Joseph Rowntree Foundation Inquiry into Income and Wealth*, Vol. 1, York: Joseph Rowntree Foundation, 1995. Hills, J., *Joseph Rowntree Foundation Inquiry into Income and Wealth*, Vol. 2, York: Joseph Rowntree Foundation, 1995.

7   Dennis, N., *The Invention of Permanent Poverty*, London: IEA Health and Welfare Unit, 1997, chapters 3 and 4.

8   Guilty figures for 1954 are taken from *Crime Statistics England and Wales 1954*, Table III and Tables VII–X. Guilty figures for 1994 are taken from *Crime Statistics England and Wales 1994*, Tables 5.13–5.21 and unpublished breakdowns provided by the Home Office.

9   Clear-up data for 1954 come from *Crime Statistics England and Wales 1954*, Table I. Clear-up data for 1994 are taken from *Crime Statistics England and Wales 1994*, Table 2.8 and Table 2.15–2.21.

2: The American Experiment in Imprisonment

1   Prison data are taken from Bureau of the Census, *Statistical Abstract of the United States 1995*, Washington: Government Printing Office, Table 389, and comparable tables in earlier volumes. Crime data are taken from Federal Bureau of Investigation, *Uniform Crime Reports 1995*, Washington: Government Printing Office, Table 1, and comparable tables in earlier volumes.

2   Reynolds, M.O., *Crime in Texas*, Dallas: National Center for Policy Analysis, 1991.

3   Levitt, S.D., 'The Effect of Prison Population Size on Crime Rates: Evidence from Prison Over-crowding Litigation', *Quarterly Journal of Economics*, Vol. 3, 1996, pp. 319-52.

4   Marvell, T.B. and Moody Jr., C.E., 'Prison Population Growth and Crime Reduction', *Journal of Quantitative Criminology*, Vol. 10, no. 2, 1994, p. 136.

5   Langan, P.A., 'Between Prison and Probation: Intermediate Sanctions', *Science*, Vol. 264, May 1994, p. 791. See also Langan, P.A., 'America's Soaring Prison Population', *Science*, Vol. 251, March 1991, p. 1573.

6   Data in this discussion are taken from Bennett, W.J., DiIulio Jr., J.J. and Walters, J.P., *Body Count: Moral Poverty...And How to Win America's War Against Crime and Drugs*, New York: Simon & Schuster, 1996, chapter 3.

7   DiIulio Jr., J.J., 'Prisons are a Bargain, By Any Measure', *New York Times*, 16 January 1996, p. A17.

3: Making Prison Work

1   Author's interview, August 1996.

2   Faulkner, D., 'All Flaws and Disorder', *The Guardian*, date TK, 1996, p. TK. [Emphasis added.]

3   The most accessible version of the 'broken windows' presentation is Wilson, J.Q., *Thinking about Crime*, New York: Basic Books, 1975, chapter 5.

4   Bratton, W.J., 'Crime is Down in New York City: Blame the Police', in Dennis, N. (ed.), *Zero Tolerance: Policing a Free Society*, London: IEA Health and Welfare Unit, 1997, p. 29.

5   *Crime Statistics England and Wales 1994*, Tables 5.2 and 5.9.

6   *Crime Statistics England and Wales 1954*, pp. xx and xxvii.

7   *Crime Statistics England and Wales 1954*, Tables IX and X. *Crime Statistics England and Wales 1994*, Tables 7.6 and 7.7.

Commentaries

Charles Murray and the American Prison Experiment: The Dilemmas of a Libertarian

1 Murray, C. *Losing Ground: American Social Policy 1950-1980*, New York: Basic Books, 1984.

2 Murray, C., *The Emerging British Underclass*, London: IEA Health and Welfare Unit, 1990.

3 Murray, C. and Herrnstein, R.J., *The Bell Curve: Intelligence and Class Structure in American Life*, New York: The Free Press, 1994.

4 Murray, C., *What it Means to be a Libertarian: A Personal Interpretation*, New York: Boundary Books, 1997.

5 Bureau of Justice Statistics, *Correctional Populations in the United States*, Washington DC: US Department of Justice, 1995.

6 See Currie, E., *Is America Really Winning the War on Crime and Should Britain Follow its Example?*, London: NACRO, 1996.

7 See Home Office, *Criminal Statistics, England and Wales, 1995*, London: The Stationery Office, 1996.

8 See Mauer, M., *Intended and Unintended Consequences: State Racial Disparities in Imprisonment*, Washington D: The Sentencing Project, 1997.

9 Bauman, Z., *Life in Fragments*, Oxford: Blackwells, 1995.

10 Mauer, M., *op. cit.*

Sentencing Trends and Public Confidence

1 Home Office, *Crime, Justice and Protecting the Public*, London: HMSO, 1990, p. 6.

2 Prison Commission, *Report of the Prison Commission*, London: 1955, p. 16.

3 Home Office, *Committee of Inquiry into the UK Prison Services*. London: HMSO, 1979, Figure 3.3.

4 Nuttall, C. and Pease, K., 'Changes in the Use of Imprisonment in England and Wales 1950-1991', *Criminal Law Review*, May, 1994, p. 318.

5 Davies, M., Pekka-Takkala and Tyrer, J., *Penological Esperanto and Sentencing Parochialism: A Comparative Study of the Search for Non-Prison Punishments*, Aldershot: Dartmouth, 1996.

6 Davies, M., *Punishing Criminals*. Westport: Greenwood, 1993.

Beyond Crime Control

1 Wilson, J.Q., 'Crime and Punishment in Britain' *The Public Interest*, 43, 1976, p. 5.

2 Wilson, J.Q., *Thinking About Crime*, New York: Basic Books, 1975.

3 Murray, C.A., *Losing Ground: American Social Policy, 1950-1980*, New York: Basic Books, 1984. See also Blumenthal, S., *The Rise of the Counter-Establishment: From Conservative Ideology to Political Power*, New York: Times Books, 1986. It is not entirely fair to say that Murray turned his hand to crime rather late in the day. His first and least well known book, co-authored with Cox, L., was *Beyond Probation: Juvenile Corrections and the Chronic Offender*, Beverley Hills, CA: Sage Publications, 1979.

4 Wilson, J.Q., 'On Crime and the Liberals', *Dissent*, 33, 1985, p. 223.

5 DiIulio, J.J., 'Let 'Em Rot', *The Wall Street Journal*, 26 January, 1994.

6 Wilson, J.Q. and Kelling, G.L., 'Broken Windows: The Police and Neighbourhood Safety', *The Atlantic Monthly*, 249, March 1982, pp. 29-38.

7 Christie, N., *Social Control as Industry. Towards GULAGS, Western Style*, second edition, London: Routledge, 1995.

8 See Rutherford, A., 'Criminal Policy and the Eliminative Ideal', Southampton, Institute of Criminal Justice, University of Southampton, 1996.

9 Wilson, J.Q., 'Crime and American Culture', *The Public Interest*, 70, 1983, p. 46.

10 Radzinowicz, L., 'Penal Regressions', *Cambridge Law Journal*, 50, 1991, pp. 422-44.

11 Recent statements of the socio-liberal position for American criminal policy include Currie, E., *Confronting Crime: An American Challenge*, New York: Pantheon Books, 1985; Curtis, L.A., *American Violence and Public Policy, An Update on the National Commission on the Causes and Prevention of Violence*, New Haven and London: Yale University Press, 1985; Donziger, S. (ed.), *The Real War on Crime*, Report of the National Criminal Justice Commission, New York: Harper Collins, 1996; and Miller, J.G., *Search and Destroy. African-American Males in the Criminal Justice System*, New York: Cambridge University Press, 1996.